Beautiful America's
IDAHO

Beautiful America's

IDAHO

Cheryl Landes

Beautiful America Publishing Company

Front cover: Grand Mogul in the Sawtooth Wilderness Area above Redfish Lake Marina

Opposite title page: Lake Pend Oreille, north Idaho

Published by
Beautiful America Publishing Company
P.O. Box 244
Woodburn, OR 97071

Library of Congress Cataloging-in-Publication Data
Landes, Cheryl, 1959-
Beautiful America's Idaho / Cheryl Landes
p. cm.
ISBN 0-89802-739-X ISBN 0-89802-738-1 (paperback)
1. Idaho–Pictorial works. 2. Idaho–Description and travel
I. Title: Idaho. II. Title.
F747 .L36 2001   979.6–dc21   2001025735

Printed in Korea

Contents

Granite Dome near Harrison Peak in the Selkirk Mountains of northern Idaho

St. Joe River, Panhandle National Forest

Copper Falls, Kaniksu National Forest

Introduction

"...If you pushed me up against a wall as to my favorite spot, I would probably answer the Rocky Mountains of the West, around Idaho. There's something about coming around a corner and seeing a meadow full of wildflowers."

—Charles Kuralt, former host of "Sunday Morning" on CBS

"...I like Idaho. The crystal streams. The rushing rivers. The forests. The mountains. The lakes as blue as paint. The splash of mountain ash or maple. The foam of the syringa, the state's official flower. The awesome wastes. The fruitful fields. The warm friendliness of crossroads and town. The high sky over it all."

—A.B. Guthrie, author of *The Big Sky*

Although Idaho's nickname, "The Gem State," refers to her vast mineral resources, the name could be more appropriately applied to her beautiful, diverse landscape. Her elevations range from 738 to 12,662 feet above sea level. She has wild, rushing rivers and the tallest sand dunes in America. She's the most mountainous of every Rocky Mountain state with more than 80 ranges, yet has the Treasure and Emmett Valleys, agricultural paradises yielding among the most bountiful harvests in the country. More than 40 peaks tower at over 10,000 feet, while the Snake River rumbles through Hells Canyon, the deepest gorge on the continent. There are the golden wheat fields of the Palouse country and the bustling metropolis of Boise, the state's capital and largest city. Mineral springs gush above ground, and crystal ice caves burrow under her surface. And her history continues to live on in the ghost towns, abandoned mining camps, and remnants of the Oregon and California Trails.

Last but not least, she's genuinely hospitable. As Linda Stirling wrote in the last edition of this book, "The people of Idaho are a friendly bunch, eager to share the bounty of their region. When you stop in for a burger and slice of pie at a roadside cafe, you're likely to get the cook's recipe for lemon meringue and the fellow at the counter will offer directions to his favorite fishing spot." Some of my best adventures in the state have been discovered by talking to the locals, and I eagerly await many more.

Wild rose along the Kootenai River by Bonners Ferry

North Idaho

North Idaho, also called the Panhandle, has the greatest concentration of lakes of any western state. Some are among the country's largest, others are the most scenic, while still others are remote and intimate.

Since the late 1980s, Lake Coeur d'Alene has grown into a popular vacation spot with its busy waterfront and luxurious resorts. It's no wonder; after all, *National Geographic* magazine named the sapphire marvel surrounded by mountains and lush forest one of the five most beautiful in the world. The lake stretches 25 miles and averages 2.5 miles wide. One of the nation's largest populations of ospreys nest here in the spring, and during the winter, bald eagles pluck salmon from the waters of Wolf Lodge Bay.

One of the trendiest places here is The Coeur d'Alene Resort on the lake's north shore in downtown Coeur d'Alene with its spectacular views, boardwalk, and world-famous floating green. The resort is so popular that if you want to book a room during the peak seasons, make plans *at least* six months in advance. Shop for hand-crafted arts and crafts at the resort or in the downtown shops, or take a tour in a horse-drawn carriage, double-decker bus, boat, or seaplane.

Lake Pend Orielle in Sandpoint is one of the largest freshwater lakes in the Pacific Northwest and has a depth of 1,150 feet. The lake attracts fishermen who hope to hook some Kamloops rainbow trout during the special fishing season from early May through late November. Other popular activities include swimming, boating, picnicking, and a two-hour guided boat tour of the lake. The Fourth of July fireworks display over the lake is spectacular, and The Festival at Sandpoint is a popular summer concert series.

My favorite place in Sandpoint is the Cedar Street Bridge Public Market, formerly the city bridge across Sand Creek. The renovated rustic two-level structure is an enclosed covered bridge with abundant windows and a lush assortment of greenery, modeled after the Ponte Vecchio bridge shops in Florence, Italy. Shops include Coldwater Creek Catalog Company, an assortment of smaller arts and crafts shops and carts, and numerous eateries.

Priest Lake, north of Sandpoint, cannot be reached by any major highway, and many of the campsites here along the 72-mile shoreline with dense ferns, spruce, and hemlock can only be accessed by boat. Canoeing, boating, fishing, and hiking are among the many adventures you can experience in this place of quiet solitude—the perfect getaway from it all.

Skiing is a favorite winter sport at Schweitzer Mountain, 11 miles northwest of Sandpoint. Long before a resort opened here in 1963, the adventurous tied skis to their backs and snowshoes to their feet and hiked to the top at 6,400 feet. Their quest brought rewards few people knew—the boldness of standing far above the rest of the world, the stunning panoramas, and the thrill and freedom of plowing through knee-deep powder in a place relatively unexplored.

Today's skiers don't have to hike up this peak, but they can still experience the excitement, beauty, and uncrowded surroundings cherished by their earlier counterparts. Up to 25 feet (300 inches) of the Northwest's driest snow cover two natural bowls totaling 2,350 acres. Forty-eight runs of varying difficulty cross glades filled with the aroma of ponderosa pine or open spaces with unobstructed views of the Selkirk Mountains, Lake Pend Orielle, and Montana's Cabinet Range. Anyone standing on the peak of Schweitzer is enveloped by the powerful scenery and suddenly feels like a small part of the universe.

Harbor Resorts, the owners of Stevens Pass and Mission Ridge ski areas in Washington, recently purchased Schweitzer Mountain Ski Resort and have added a host of improvements, including expanded beginner ski areas, a bigger snowboard park, and two new handle tows. The former Green Gables Lodge has also been extensively renovated and renamed the Selkirk Lodge.

In the summer, Schweitzer comes alive with colorful wildflowers. You can ride the

Harvested field near Bonners Ferry frames Black Mountain in the Cabinet Mountains of northern Idaho

The Old Mission at Cataldo

chairlift to the top of the mountain, enjoy a family picnic, pick wild huckleberries, rent a mountain bike, or hike the Schweitzer Nature Trail to secluded mountain lakes and streams.

Silver Mountain Ski Resort is the end of an incredible story of how a town managed to make a remarkable recovery after an economic disaster that could have otherwise turned the community into a ghost town. From the late 1880s until the early 1980s, Kellogg was known as one of the largest silver-mining communities in the United States. Silver was its major industry until the early 1980s, after the metal rose to its highest price ever and then dove dramatically. Closure of the mines in 1981 was followed by an abrupt collapse of the economy and a quiet exodus by many residents.

But those who remained behind possessed the tenacity needed to save this town. In 1985, Wayne Ross, former senior city councilman, started planning an ambitious project— building a gondola to the top of Kellogg Peak, the site of the old Silverhorn skiing area in the Bitterroot Mountain Range. A group of his friends was soon meeting at his office at six every morning to try to make this dream a reality. They felt the project would attract tourists and boost Kellogg's economy.

Shortly before Christmas 1987, a $6.4 million grant became available. However, there was one catch—the city of Kellogg was required to raise matching funds by a September 30, 1988 deadline. Meetings and negotiations with potential investors began in an attempt to acquire the money, but as time passed, hope faded.

Finally, just before the deadline, a supporter stepped forward with partial funding, and the citizens of Kellogg provided the rest by approving an additional property tax on September 28, 1988.

The results of this hard work produced Silver Mountain Resort, which opened in 1990. Since then, the resort has become one of the most popular in the Pacific Northwest. Over 2,000 acres of terrain stretch across the resort's basins formed by twin peaks Kellogg and Wardner. The area's summit rises to 6,300 feet, dropping to a base area of 4,000 feet. The

Beauty Bay, Lake Coeur d'Alene

Bitterroot Mountains receive an average annual snowfall of over 200 inches, and wonderful powder skiing. There are 44 trails and 2,200 vertical feet of skiing, ranging from wide-open, gentle tours for beginners, to steep challenges for those with more experience.

The ski area is accessed by the Alpine Express, the world's longest single-stage gondola, stretching 3.1 miles and rising 3,400 vertical feet from the base terminal in Kellogg to the upper terminal. The gondola, constructed by VonRoll Transport Systems of Geneva, Switzerland, consists of over 100 enclosed, eight-passenger cabins, which transport visitors from the base village to the upper terminal in approximately 16 minutes.

The ride to the top of Kellogg Peak is an event in itself. The Alpine Express crosses over the town of Kellogg, where the remnants of its mining history are still visible in the older homes, businesses, and abandoned mines. Scars left in the surrounding hills also reveal where miners removed silver.

As the gondola rises higher, the buildings turn into small patches, then dots, and finally disappear as a larger, panoramic alpine view unfolds. Below the gondola, passengers can watch skiers descend on Kellogg Peak's trails and may even catch a glimpse of deer or rabbit tracks in the snow.

Summer is just as much fun at Silver Mountain. From June to September, activities include riding the Alpine Express, enjoying Western barbecues and picnics on the Mountain Haus' sundeck, and exploring nature paths. Live dramatic, theatrical, and musical presentations are scheduled throughout the season at a natural mountain amphitheater, which seats 3,000 people.

Views of three states (Washington, Idaho, and Montana) and Canada from fields carpeted with wildflowers await summer visitors. For the more adventuresome, hiking trails and a network of mountain bike trails weave through the area's peaks and valleys, featuring a downhill coast from the Mountain Haus to the base village in Kellogg. The scenery in the fall is beautiful, too, when the tamaracks and aspens reveal their golden hues.

Skiers who prefer a more remote setting will enjoy Lookout Pass east of Wallace near the Idaho-Montana border.

Wallace is at the junction of four major canyons, three of which lead into active mines of the Coeur d'Alene Mining District. Although sagging silver prices in the 1980s closed several mines in the area, Wallace remains a major lead and silver producer. Despite the decline, the Coeur d'Alene Mining District is still among the top 10 silver producers in the world. Seven of the top 25 United States silver mines are here, and operations are conducted as far as 3,000 feet below sea level. Some of the mines founded in the late 1800s now have 200 miles of tunnels. The district is also the all-time leader in silver production; approximately one billion ounces have been removed since Colonel Wallace settled there in 1884.

The Old West spirit has not left the town of 1,000, either. Hardy, independent residents share a camaraderie that only those living in a hardrock mining town can understand. It is a characteristic that will last for years to come.

Hollywood has used Wallace as a backdrop for its movies, because it has the best preserved 19th century architecture and the entire town is on the National Register of Historic Places. Once you're inside the city limits, you feel as though you've been whisked back to the late 1800s. The beautifully restored Northern Pacific Depot Railroad Museum houses a re-creation of an early 1900s railroad depot and exhibits telling the story of the railroading history of the Coeur d'Alene mining district. The Sixth Street Melodrama offers plays and musicals in the summer, February, April, and November. The highlight is family-style melodrama that depicts the area's mining heritage, followed by the Kelly's Alley Revue of old-fashioned music and humor. Audience participation is strongly encouraged.

A number of smaller working and abandoned mining communities are north of Wallace. Stop by the visitor's center in downtown Wallace and pick up a map for a self-guided tour. Not only will you get a taste of northern Idaho's mining history, but you'll also be treated to views of rolling hills, mountains, and pine forests. You can also get a close-up look at

Dworshak Dam, Orofino

Deep Creek, Hells Canyon National Recreation Area, Seven Devils Mountains

mining operations by taking the guided tour of the Sierra Silver Mine. Many of the guides used to work the mines in the district.

You can also bike on the world's largest trail system (1,000 miles) across open meadows, high mountain ridges, and deep canyons. Don't miss the Route of Hiawatha, a 13-mile trail that runs on a former railbed through nine tunnels and seven trestle bridges. It has spectacular vistas and, best of all, it's mostly downhill.

Another historic highlight is the mission at Cataldo, between Coeur d'Alene and Kellogg. In 1847, Father Jean de Smet, Jesuit missionaries, and the Coeur d'Alene Indians built the "Mission of the Sacred Heart" with wooden pegs, straw, and river mud on a grassy hill above the Coeur d'Alene River. The lemon-yellow structure is the oldest building still standing in Idaho. A visitor's center has displays and a short slide show about the history of the mission and the lives of the missionaries and Indians who worshipped there.

Bonners Ferry is known as "the last frontier in the contiguous USA." Three mountain ranges circle the town, which straddles the Kootenai River. The setting has become a natural base for fishermen, whitewater rafters, and boaters, as well as a popular starting point for hikers, horsepacking trips, and snowmobilers in the winter.

The grasslands and marshes of the Kootenai National Wildlife Refuge along the south shore of the Kootenai River is the feeding, resting, and breeding grounds for migratory birds; the most common are tundra swan in the spring and Canada geese and ducks in the fall. White-tailed and mule deer, moose, black bears, and coyotes are often spotted. Farmers grow wheat and barley in the refuge. A portion of the crops is left each year for the wildlife; the rest is harvested. An early morning stroll along the 1.5-mile Island Pond Wildlife Trail is a good chance to see some of the wildlife.

Highway 2, the scenic route to Montana's Glacier National Park departs Bonners Ferry. Between mileposts 70 and 71 is an overlook of the Moyie River canyon, Moyie Falls, and the Big Moyie Canyon Bridge. The bridge is one of Idaho's highest at over 600 feet above the canyon.

North Central Idaho

North Central Idaho is another region of stunning contrasts. Upon first glance, it appears to be an uninhabited land of mountains, canyons, and rivers. But people are here and manage to live in harmony with the untamed beauty that surrounds them. Endless ridges of evergreens border the Palouse country outside Moscow, one of the largest wheat-producing areas in the United States. The words, "amber waves of grain," from the song, "America the Beautiful," best describe the scene of miles of amber wheat fields dancing in the breeze. Bright yellow canola and green pea and lentil fields, along with brown plowed tracts of soil awaiting planting, contribute patches of color to this giant breadbasket. The occasional red barn, silo, and farmhouse in the background resemble tiny game pieces on a huge game board.

Only Alaska has more wilderness than Idaho's 18 million preserved acres, and many are found in the North Central region: the Selway-Bitterroot Wilderness, the Gospel Hump Wilderness, the Frank Church River of No Return Wilderness Area, the Payette National Forest, and the Mallard-Larkins Pioneer Area. Hells Canyon, America's deepest river gorge, stretches for 70 miles along the Snake River between the Idaho-Oregon Border. The mighty Seven Devils Mountains form a semicircle one and one-half miles above the canyon. Thirty alpine lakes are scattered throughout the rugged peaks—a pristine haven for hikers, backpackers, and horseback riders. The lakes are accessible from the trails at Windy Saddle Camp, two miles below Heaven's Gate.

Although you can see Hells Canyon from several viewpoints, the best is Heaven's Gate Lookout on Forest Road 517. The gravel road turns off from Highway 95, one mile south of Riggins. The setting makes anyone feel like he or she is in heaven with the seemingly endless panorama of most of the canyon and parts of Oregon, Washington, Montana, and

Hells Canyon of the Snake River

Wilson and Harbor lakes, Big Horn Crags in the River of No Return Wilderness Area

the Central Idaho Rockies. Occasionally the elusive downy-white mountain goat can be spotted on the crags of the Seven Devils.

For a more close-up, personal experience with the canyon, sign up for one of the guided jet boat or float trips out of Lewiston. Tours range from one to five days.

More river adventures can be had from the town of Riggins, the area's whitewater capital at the junction of the Little Salmon and main Salmon Rivers. Several outfitters offer jet boat and raft trips that glide past abandoned mines, fishing camps, Indian burial grounds, and petroglyphs. In the early morning and evening, elk, deer, goats, and dozens of species of birds feed along the shore.

Two more challenging rivers in this area are the Selway and Lochsa. The latter parallels Highway 12, which roughly follows the original route of Meriwether Lewis and William Clark through miles of pristine forest and eventually into the Nez Perce National Historic Park. Despite the closeness of the highway, rafters will barely notice its presence. Lewis and Clark almost perished here while crossing the Bitterroot Mountains over the Lolo Trail. The Nez Perce saved them just in time, and the grateful leaders of the expedition remembered the tribe as the most hospitable people of the journey.

You can also float the rivers in your own boat, but if you choose this option, plan ahead of time. Often permits are required if you don't schedule a trip through an outfitter. A limited number are available, so you must apply several months in advance.

After returning to Riggins from your whitewater adventure, spend some time at the Rapid River Fish Hatchery, one of the Northwest's most successful Chinook salmon breeding operations. Or carry a fishing pole and some bait to one of the nearby dams. The reservoirs at Oxbow, Brownlee, and Hells Canyon dams offer easy access to more than 19,000 acres of prime fishing, water skiing, and boating areas. There's also Dworshak Dam, the largest straight-axis dam in North America with a 54-mile tree-lined shore along its reservoir. Dam tours, lake cruises, and houseboat rentals are also available at Dworshak.

Another choice fishing spot is at the lake in Winchester State Park, where you can rent a yurt for the night. While you're there, stop at the Wolf Education and Research Center, where you'll see gray wolves in their natural habitat on a self-guided tour and learn more about these magnificent creatures at the exhibits in the visitor's center.

Two of the state's best museums are in North Central Idaho. St. Gertrude's, overlooking the Camas Prairie near Cottonwood, has an extensive collection of artifacts left by Polly Bemis who came to the area as a Chinese slave. Her story is told in the movie, "A Thousand Pieces of Gold," and the book bearing the same name. There are also relics from Buckskin Bill, a modern mountain man who made his own tools and guns, along with rare Oriental and European antique furniture and ceramics, a baby bottle for twins, and horse snowshoes. The sisters who live at the St. Gertrude's convent are the best museum guides you'll find anywhere.

The museum at the Nez Perce National Historic Park is a wonderful place to get a sense of this tribe's culture. View the collection of artifacts, and then take a look at the other sites in the park: the Indian Agency dating back to 1861, Idaho's first homestead, a Presbyterian church built in the 1880s, the Poor Coyote cabin, and the Spalding Mission Cemetery. A number of interesting geologic formations named after animals are around Spalding, including Coyote's Fishnet, The Bear, and Ant and Yellowjacket.

Northwest of Spalding, the Clearwater and Snake Rivers meet at Lewiston, the site where Lewis and Clark camped in 1805 on their way to Oregon and again in 1806 on the return East. Later, when gold was discovered nearby, Lewiston became a supply post for the mining camps and served briefly as the capital of Idaho. Today, the town of 28,000 is an inland seaport, where ships dock after a 465-mile journey from the Pacific Ocean up the Snake and Columbia Rivers. The Luna House Museum on Third and C Streets features displays of American Indian and pioneer artifacts and is an excellent example of art deco architecture.

View of Sawtooth Range from Boise National Forest

A transition in the scenery comes at Lewiston, where rolling hills and fertile valleys replace the towering mountains and deep canyons. To get a bird's eye perspective of it all, take US 95 north to the viewpoint at the top of Lewiston Hill.

The other major commercial center in the region is Moscow, where the harvests of the Palouse are processed and distributed throughout the United States. The town was a favorite summer destination for the Nez Perce and trapping ground for the French Canadians in the early 1800s. During the 1860s, it became a base camp during the gold rush and is also known as the home of the Appaloosa horse.

Moscow is home to the state's oldest university, the University of Idaho, which evokes a feeling of a New England college town with its stained-glass windows and Gothic dormitories dating back to the late 1880s. Exhibits of rocks and minerals in the Life Science and College of Mines buildings are open to visitors, as is the USDA Intermountain Forest and Range Experiment Station, a joint effort of the university and the U.S. Forest Service in researching ways to prevent disease and insect damage to white pines.

For a truly unique rockhounding experience, go to the Emerald Creek Garnet Area in the St. Joe National Forest south of St. Maries. Here at 281 Gulch, you can dig for star garnets while watching butterflies flutter among the wildflowers sprinkled across green meadows surrounded by giant ponderosa pines. The only sounds, other than your shovel scooping up mud and rocks from the streambed, are those of the trickling creek and songbirds chirping in the trees. You'll need your own equipment to dig, but you can purchase permits at the site, which allow you to remove up to five pounds of garnets.

Southwestern Idaho

Mother Nature has assembled quite a collection of valleys in Southwestern Idaho. There's Long Valley and Round Valley, named for their shapes; Bear Valley, known for its bears; and Duck Valley, a favorite feeding ground for waterfowl. There's also Garden Valley and Meadows Valley, both appropriately named for their picture postcard settings. And then there's Treasure Valley and Emmett Valley in their idyllic agricultural settings. At the heart of it all is Boise, Idaho's largest city, the state capital, and a place ranked among America's most livable cities.

The City of Trees was founded in 1863 to serve the miners in the nearby hills and later became a trading center for the immigrants traveling west on the Oregon Trail. Today, the quality of life, low cost of living, and liberal tax incentives have attracted many national and multinational headquarters to the city of 125,000, including Boise Cascade, Albertsons, Hewlett-Packard, Micron Technology, and T.J. International. Light industry also thrives here, especially high-tech. Even Furby had its origins here. Tiger Electronics, the makers of the interactive furball, purchased the licensing rights from Boise toy inventor Caleb Chung. And, characteristic of the other major cities in the Pacific Northwest, you can ski or fish in the morning, play a game of tennis or golf in the afternoon, savor a gourmet meal at an award-winning restaurant in the evening, and then enjoy the ballet, opera, or Shakespeare play.

There's much more to do here. Shop and eat in historic Hyde Park on 13th Street, stroll the Art and Cultural District, or take a guided tour of the Idaho Statehouse. This sandstone structure with a beautiful marble interior is heated with geothermal water and contains a number of interesting displays, monuments, and artifacts about Idaho's past.

The city's centerpiece is the 25-mile greenbelt along the Boise River, the home of the

Bruneau River Canyon, southwest Idaho

Bruneau Dunes State Park, south of Mountain Home

Kathryn Albertson Natural Park, Julia Davis Park, and an extensive network of bicycle and walking trails. In Julia Davis Park, you'll find the Idaho Historical Museum, the nationally renowned Boise Art Museum, Zoo Boise, and the Idaho Black History Museum, which is celebrating more than 100 years of contributions from the state's African Americans.

Other attractions include the Boise Tour Train, Basque Museum and Cultural Center, Ann Morrison Park, Idaho Botanical Garden, Old Idaho Penitentiary, Morrison Knudsen Nature Center, the Idaho Botanical Garden, and the World Center for Birds of Prey. Popular seasonal activities include The Idaho Shakespeare Festival in the summer and skiing at Bogus Basin Resort in the winter.

Southwestern Idaho has a variety of festivals offering something for everyone: the National Oldtime Fiddlers' Contest in Weiser, the Apple Blossom Festival in Payette, the Cherry Festival in Emmett, and Horseshoe Days in New Plymouth.

McCall, an old sawmill town on the southern shore of Payette Lake, is a popular year-round resort. Golf, shopping, gourmet restaurants, hunting, fishing, horseback riding, camping, boating, water skiing, and whitewater rafting are among the many activities this down-home community of 2,000 has to offer. Brundage Mountain Ski Resort attracts couples and families for skiing and snowmobiling. An ice sculpture competition is the highlight of the 10-day McCall Winter Carnival in February.

South of McCall lies the Cascade Reservoir and the town of Cascade. The reservoir, more than 20 miles long, is well stocked for fishing and surrounded by more than 20 public and private recreation areas. Waterskiers and windsurfers are also a common sight here.

History still lives on in some of the region's former mining towns. After gold and silver were discovered in the Boise Basin in 1862, Idaho City became the largest city in the Pacific Northwest and mined more gold than all of Alaska. Three years later, it was the home of approximately 7,000 miners, including one-quarter Chinese. Now 300 people live here among the well-preserved canteens and storefronts. Highlights among the 20 rustic

Balsamroot along the Middle Fork of the Boise River, Boise Mountains, Boise National Forest

Ponderosa pine near Bogus Basin in Boise Mountains looking west to Willow Ridge in West Mountains

buildings include the First Masonic Hall, the partially restored first prison of Idaho Territory, and the Boise Basin Museum, which formerly served as the post office and Wells Fargo station. Of the 200 men and women buried in the cemetery at Boot Hill, only 28 are believed to have died from natural causes.

After your tour of Idaho City, take a dip in the thermal swimming pool at Warm Springs Resort, one and one-half miles southwest of town. The resort has hot springs averaging 110 degrees Fahrenheit.

Another superb historical tour can be found high in the Owyhee Mountains at Silver City, the "Queen of Idaho Ghost Towns," where more than 75 of its original buildings remain intact. The museums in the schoolhouse, drugstore, and the 20-bedroom Idaho Hotel, Our Lady of Tears Catholic Church, and the cemeteries give visitors a first-hand experience of what life was like during the gold and silver rushes of the late 1800s.

An annual reenactment at Glenns Ferry recalls the struggles the pioneers traveling the Oregon Trail faced traversing the Snake River. At Three Island Crossing State Park, the most treacherous crossing on the Oregon Trail, wheel ruts from the covered wagons that passed through here are still visible.

South of Mountain Home at Bruneau Dunes State Park, climb North America's tallest single-structured sand dune rising over 470 feet above the desert floor, get a close-up look at local flora and fauna at the Interpretive Center, or stay after dusk on weekends to gaze at the heavens through Idaho's largest telescope at the Bruneau Dunes Observatory. The lakes below the dunes are brimming with largemouth bass and bluegill, and in the waters of the Bruneau Canyon south of the dunes. Petroglyphs drawn by the Paiute Indians can still be seen in the canyon and on the rock slabs throughout the desert.

Like North Central Idaho, the Snake River Canyon is another dominant feature of Southwestern Idaho's landscape. Here, at the Snake River Birds of Prey National Conservation Area, the almost constant updrafts allow rare raptors to hunt the desert floor and thrive as nowhere else in the world.

Several scenic drives provide spectacular views of Southwestern Idaho. Breathtaking panoramas of the Snake River are the highlights of the narrow, winding 22-mile Hells Canyon Scenic Byway. The Owyhee Uplands Backcountry Byway is a 101-mile gravel road crossing remote high desert, gnarled junipers, and sheer red river canyons. The 111-mile Payette River Scenic Byway follows the river of the same name and passes through Smiths Ferry and Cascade Lake before reaching the resort town of McCall and Payette Lake, where snow-capped peaks reflect on the glassy waters. The 130.9-mile Ponderosa Pine Scenic Byway starts in Stanley and continues through the heart of the Stanley Basin, the South Fork of the Payette River, Idaho City, and ends at Boise. Wildlife watching from several viewpoints, rafting, fishing, soaking in hot springs, and views of the turbulent South Fork of the Payette River are the highlights of the drive along the Wildlife Canyon Scenic Byway.

Payette Lake, North Beach State Park

Moon over Payette Lake

Idaho State Capitol, Boise

Central Idaho

Central Idaho could be easily mistaken for the Swiss Alps with its abundance of rugged ranges: the Boulders, White Clouds, Sawtooths, Bitterroots, and Lost River. It's also home of the state's highest peak, Mount Borah, towering 12,662 feet north of Arco. In 1983, a large earthquake raised the mountain two feet while lowering the valley below by five feet. Literally thousands of alpine lakes are nestled among the peaks and as many creeks flow to the sweeping plains and prairies below where elk, deer, moose, and antelope graze.

Add abundant snowfall to this magnificent setting, and you have the makings of a world-class ski destination. That's exactly what happened in 1936, when Averell Harriman asked Austrian Count Felix Schaffgotsch to find a site for a resort in the western United States "of the same character as the Swiss and Austrian Alps." The result was Sun Valley, the nation's first destination ski resort which quickly pioneered the world's first chairlift and became a popular hangout for international celebrities, such as Ernest Hemingway, Clark Gable, Ingrid Bergman, Gary Cooper, and Marilyn Monroe. Despite its origins, though, Sun Valley and its neighbor, Ketchum, have evolved into a year-round vacation haven with activities for the entire family, ranging from shopping in the resort's cozy Old World style village to sports such as ice skating, swimming, tennis, and golf. And, of course, the skiing at the resort's 78 runs remains the top attraction in the winter.

The only three routes into the town of Stanley have been designated scenic byways: the Ponderosa Pine Scenic Byway, Salmon River Scenic Byway, and Sawtooth Scenic Byway. Stanley is a favorite jumping off point for hikers, backpackers, and horseback riders to the Sawtooth Wilderness and Sawtooth National Recreation Areas, and put-in point for float trips on the Middle Fork of the Salmon River. The tiny town of 100 stands alongside the Salmon River on the north edge of the Stanley Basin—a great mountain meadow sprinkled with cattle ranches, lodgepole pine forests, guest lodges, and campgrounds.

It's no wonder the Sawtooth National Recreation Area attracts so many outdoor enthusiasts with its rivers, streams, and more than 300 alpine lakes in its lodgepole pine forests. Outstanding trout fishing, sailing, and boating can be found in the five lower lakes of the Sawtooth Wilderness: Alturas, Petit, Little Redfish, Redfish, and Stanley.

More rafting adventures can be found at Salmon City, the former winter campsite of Jim Bridger and Kit Carson. This "whitewater capital of the world" sits at the forks of the Salmon and Lemhi Rivers close to the edge of the Salmon Valley, known for its cattle ranches and timber. Here outfitters run the main Salmon River, nicknamed "The River of No Return" by Lewis and Clark. The name is appropriate, for the Salmon is one of the few remaining undammed waterways in the United States. The river and its forks are the only pathways into the River of No Return Wilderness Area, the country's largest single wilderness.

Two excellent fishing spots are in Central Idaho. Rainbow trout weighing up to five pounds and brown trout as large as 12 pounds are abundant at Mormon and Magic Reservoirs near Fairfield. Silver Creek, one of Ernest Hemingway's favorite places for fly-fishing, flows southeast of Bellevue.

Yankee Fork Historic Loop starts at Challis and continues for 91 miles through old stage stations, ghost towns like Bonanza, abandoned mines and mills, and a gold dredge and tailings. Tours of the dredge are offered in the summer. At the interpretive center in Challis, an 18-minute slide show, dioramas, and photographs tell the story of the ghost towns, mines, and miners living in the area from 1860 through 1910. Salmon spawn in August and September at the Indian Riffles Salmon Spawning Grounds near Sunbeam.

Craters of the Moon National Monument is the most unusual volcanic formation in Idaho. The craters and cave resemble the surface of the moon and are part of a 60-mile-long crack in the earth's crust where eruptions occurred as late as 2,100 years ago. Along the

Bighorn ram

View od Sawtooth Range from Park Creek Meadow

Opposite: Sawtooth Mountains and Big Wood River, Sawtooth National Recreation Area

seven-mile loop road, the colors of the hardened lava change suddenly from black to rust and back again. Short hikes provide opportunities to look inside the vent of a cinder cone, cross the surface of a lava flow, and explore an icy lava tube. In the winter, the loop road is groomed into a Nordic ski trail.

Nearby, Arco was America's first city to be powered with electricity generated from nuclear power in 1955, thanks to its close proximity to the Idaho National Engineering and Environmental Laboratories of the U.S. Department of Energy. The EBR-1 National Historic Landmark, east of Arco off Highway 20, offers a safe, educational overview of the development of nuclear energy.

The Lewis and Clark Backcountry Byway wanders 39 miles through stands of firs and pines, rolling hills, and mountain meadows. The setting looks about the same today as in 1805, when the famous expedition leaders climbed to the top of Lemhi Pass and unfurled the US flag for the first time in the West.

Eastern Idaho

Like its neighbors, Yellowstone and Teton National Parks, Eastern Idaho shares the same awesome beauty but lacks the crowds. There are roaring waterfalls, peaceful lakes, rushing rivers, and the snow-capped peaks of the Grand Tetons, the youngest mountains in the Rockies at barely 10 million years old rising as high as 13,722 feet. There are grasslands where elk, moose, deer, and antelope graze while eagles soar high on the fresh breezes. And there's Grand Targhee Resort east of Driggs, which has some of the best powder skiing you'll find anywhere.

Upper and Lower Mesa Falls on State Highway 47 are the last undisturbed waterfalls along the Snake River. At Lower Mesa Falls, the Snake River squeezes into a gorge dropping 65 feet. The best place to see this natural phenomenon is from the Grandview Campground and overlook. From the campground, you can also hear waters of the upper falls, which whip up a mist as they plunge 114 feet, the equivalent of the height of an 11-story building.

Henry's Fork of the Snake River, recognized by fly fishermen as one of the best in the world, is only a few miles from the Continental Divide at Targhee Pass. The stream continues through Harriman State Park in the heart of Island Park, 4,330 acres of high-country meadows and pristine forests. It's also the center of a 16,000-acre wildlife refuge best known for its large concentration of trumpeter swans. Guides offer tours of the rustic buildings of the Railroad Ranch, which was formerly owned by the Harriman family of the Union Pacific Railroad. Groomed cross-country ski trails crisscross the park in the winter.

The drive to Island Park is outstanding. The road from Ashton through the Upper Snake River Valley climbs the edge of an ancient caldera—a collapsed volcano 18 miles long and 23 miles wide, with a 1,200-foot scarp on the south and west rims. At the top, there's a

Looking south to Saddle Mountain, crest of Lemhi Range, Challis National Forest

Bowery Peak and East Pass Creek drainage from Hunter Pass, Boulder Mountains

panorama of rolling hills surrounded by mountains.

At Idaho Falls, the highways separate. I-15 departs into Montana, US 20 enters Yellowstone, and US 26 crosses the Grand Tetons. Originally founded in 1860 as Taylor's Crossing, the town attracted miners traveling to Montana from Salt Lake City. After the gold rushes ended and many of the residents departed for greener pastures, those left behind were faced with adopting a new livelihood or surrendering the town to the list of growing ghost towns in the West. They decided to dig irrigation ditches to turn the arid land, and the area rapidly transformed into a tapestry of gold and green croplands. Today nearly 44,000 people live here, and the irrigation system that saved the town provides water to over one million acres of crops. Attractions include more than 30 parks, including Tautphaus Park with its nationally-renowned zoo; the Bonneville Museum; the Idaho Vietnam Memorial; and the 14-mile Snake River Greenbelt, which passes the roaring falls sharing the city's name and the Latter Day Saints Temple. A picnic area overlooks the falls.

North of Idaho Falls is Bear World, a wildlife park where black bears, grizzlies, elk, reindeer, and fallow deer, thrive in their natural habitats.

Idaho Falls isn't the only town in Eastern Idaho that has experienced miraculous recoveries from almost certain deaths. On June 5, 1976, the Teton Dam collapsed and dumped 80 billion gallons of water from the Snake River into the valley below. Rexburg and other valley towns were submerged, but were rebuilt after the floods receded. The collapsed dam site is still visible from an overlook just off State Highway 33, east of Newdale, and the Teton Flood Museum in Rexburg relives the dramatic disaster.

Rexburg is also the home of Ricks College, a serene, private college established in 1888, and the Idaho International Folk Dance Festival, a week-long event in August that features some of the best dance groups from around the world.

Dune buggy and off-road vehicle fans will love riding the St. Anthony Sand Dunes north of the town of St. Anthony. The dunes, which contain quartz sand, were created by the prevailing winds that blew for millions of years across the Snake River plain. The dunes cover an area 35 miles long by five miles wide, and many are higher than those found in California's Death Valley.

Sawtooth Lake frames Mount Regan in the Sawtooth Wilderness Area

Beaver ponds on the Big Wood River reflecting the Boulder Mountains, Sawtooth National Recreation Area

Blodgett Pass on the Bitterroot Divide, Selway - Bitterroot Wilderness

The Payette River, north of Boise

*Rafters on the Middle Fork Salmon River
River of No Return Wilderness Area*

Salmon River Canyon, River of No Return Wilderness Area

Lava flows, Craters of the Moon National Monument

Craters of the Moon National Monument

Shooting stars and common camas in full bloom in Valley Creek Meadow, Sawtooth National Forest

Bull Elk bugling in rut

Spring on the South Fork of the Clearwater River, near Grangeville

The Ram Restaurant, Sun Valley

Bald Mountain, Sun Valley Ski Area, Ketchum

Strawberry Creek drainage, Bear River Range, near the Utah border

Aspen in autumn along Targhee Creek in the Lionhead area, Targhee National Forest

Henry's Fork River near Island Park with Centennial Range beyond, Targhee National Forest

Looking across Henry's Lake from Sawtell Peak in the Centennial Mountains, the Continental Divide

City of Rocks National Reserve, south of Oakley, near the Utah border

The Snake River Canyon near Twin Falls

Perrine Bridge over the Snake River Canyon, Twin Falls

Balanced Rock near Castleford

South Central Idaho

At first, the high desert plateau of South Central Idaho may not seem like an exciting place, but in reality, it has been blessed with an abundance of unusual natural wonders, such as a rock more than 40 feet tall balancing on a base only a few feet wide, ice caves that remain frozen in the middle of summer, a river that gushes out of a canyon wall, and Shoshone Falls, 52 feet higher than the mighty Niagara straddling the U.S.-Canadian border. The best time and place to view these picturesque cascading flows of the Snake River is during the spring runoff at the south rim just outside the Twin Falls city limits.

Twin Falls is in the heart of the Magic Valley, where the Snake River irrigates 500,000 acres of farmland. The Herrett Center at the College of Southern Idaho has an elaborate collection of pre-Columbian artifacts and Hopi Kachina dolls, art galleries, a Digistar planetarium, and a Central American rainforest science camp. On the north edge of town, the Perrine Memorial Bridge spans the Snake River Gorge. The four-lane, 1,500-foot-long arch span rises 486 feet above the river and has walkways where walkers can enjoy the sweeping panorama of the gorge, Blue Lakes, and several waterfalls. One mile east of the bridge is the dirt ramp Evel Knievel used in his attempt to propel a rocket-powered motorcycle across the Snake River Canyon in 1974.

Some of the world's best bass and trout fishing can be found in the Snake River Canyon at Oster Lakes, Anderson Ponds, West Bass Ponds, Riley Creek, and Billingsly Creek.

Thirty miles northwest of Twin Falls, the Malad Gorge Canyon drops to a depth of 250 feet. A waterfall plunges 60 feet into Devils Washbowl, and can be explored from a network of trails.

The Hagerman Fossil Beds National Monument is one of the best small mammal and freshwater fish fossil sites in North America. Here scientists have removed the skeletal

Shoshone Falls on the Snake River, Twin Falls

View of 1000 Springs near Twin Falls

remains of mastodons and saber-toothed tigers, as well as extinct species of horses, camels, peccary, beavers, otters, birds, fish, and turtles in the beds aged 3.5 million years. For a more modern experience, follow the trail that overlooks the wagon train ruts of the Oregon Trail.

Parts of both the Oregon Trail and California Trail can be seen at the City of Rocks National Reserve 50 miles south of Burley. This was the turning point for many of the westward pioneers, where they had to make a decision whether to continue on to Oregon or veer south toward California. That's because the two trails parted in the backdrop of the impressive rock formations that range from 100 to 600 feet high. Today, the City of Rocks is a popular destination for rock climbers, hikers, wildlife watchers, backpackers, horseback riders, and Nordic skiers. Some of the rocks still bear the names of pioneers written in axle grease. According to legend, one of the men who robbed the Almo gold from Overland Stage in 1878 confessed on his deathbed to burying the gold near the City of Rocks.

The drive to the City of Rocks passes through Oakley, a pioneer town where an extensive assortment of elaborate stone and wood structures remain standing. The entire town is on the National Register of Historic Places and has Idaho's greatest concentration of historic buildings.

Guided tours take visitors through Shoshone Ice Cave, a 1,000-foot-long lava tube with sparkling ice crystals that are frozen year-round. Outside the cave, you'll see displays of prehistoric animals fossils that were discovered in the cave. Another place to cool off on a hot summer day is Mammoth Cave, a mile-long cavern with a variety of formations from early volcanic explosions.

Southeastern Idaho

Southeastern Idaho is a land of wide, open spaces filled with natural hot springs, geysers, and ancient caves that was once the rest area for the Oregon Trail pioneers. Today its western heritage lives on in its working cowboys, Indians in traditional dress, and architecture dating back to the late 1800s.

The region's largest city is named after the famous Shoshone, Chief Pocatello. At one time, the "Gate City" was the largest rail center west of the Mississippi River. Today, Pocatello remains the center of travel between Yellowstone National Park, Salt Lake City, Sun Valley Resort, and the rest of Idaho. Here you can stroll through Old Town, tour the three-story Oregon Short Line Depot built in the early 1900s, peek inside the wine-colored brick walls of the terra-cotta trimmed Yellowstone Hotel, or walk around the campus of Idaho State University. While at the university, don't miss the exhibits focusing on the culture of local Native Americans at the Shoshone Bannock Tribal Museum and Idaho Museum of Natural History.

Fort Hall, one of the Oregon Trail's best-known trading posts, has also been reproduced from the plans of the Hudson's Bay Company and relocated in town. A log house, drug store, and saloon are just a few of the highlights inside the fort's massive gates.

About a half hour north of Pocatello lies Blackfoot, the largest potato producing community in the world and the home of the Eastern Idaho State Fair and, naturally, the Idaho Potato Expo. American Falls Dam on the Snake River attracts fishermen, windsurfers, waterskiers, and paddleboaters.

South of Pocatello, world-renowned natural hot springs rise from the base of lava cliffs along the Portneuf River. The grounds were sacred to the Bannock and Shoshone tribes, who bathed in the hot springs to cure their ailments. They set aside the area as neutral

Snake River at Massacre Rocks State Park

Aspen along Palisades Reservoir, looking toward the Caribou Mountains, Caribou National Forest

territory and welcomed rival tribes to experience the health benefits of the mineral waters. Now a foundation of the State of Idaho operates the pool complex at Lava Hot Springs, which is open year-round and late in the evening for stargazing. Four large hot pools of the natural mineral water range in temperature from 104 to 110 degrees. There are also whirlpools, swimming pools, and diving platforms, and you can enjoy a wide variety of sports, such as golf, fishing, hunting, skiing, and snowmobiling during the winter.

Many more historical delights are scattered throughout the region. In Soda Springs, you can sample naturally carbonated water like the early pioneers and gaze at the natural captive geyser that shoots to over 100 feet. At Massacre Rocks, you can still see the deep ruts from wagon trails. Thousands of pioneers passed safely through this break in the rocks before the 1862 skirmish between local tribes and emigrants, resulting in 10 deaths. A few miles away at Register Rock, you can read the names of the pioneers carved into the rocks. The largest rock is 20 feet high and protected by a fenced enclosure in the middle of the park. Also relive the incredible journeys of the pioneers along the Oregon and California Trails by touring the living history and hands-on educational displays at the National Oregon California Trail Center in Montpelier.

South of Montpelier on Highway 89, the Romanesque Mormon Tabernacle, built in 1889, has remarkable woodworking—an excellent example of pioneer craftsmanship. Also nearby is the Monnetonka Cave, where guided tours stroll the half-mile cavern filled with stalactites, stalagmites, fossils, ice crystals, and banded travertine rock. The Bear Lake Recreation Area is a water sport center and ideal for boating. Fishing is excellent for rainbow and native cutthroat trout and the unusual Bonneville Cisco, a sardine-like whitefish that spawns with winter's frost.

Beautiful Bear Lake is by far the showcase attraction of southeastern Idaho. Tiny soluble carbonates in the water create a stunning turquoise color at midday and dazzling reds, yellows, and pinks at dawn and sunset. The lake, which is shared with Utah, is seven miles wide and 20 miles long.

Some people believe that monsters live in the lake. At the beginning of the 20th century, several sightings of strange creatures were reported here. The serpent-like creatures were said to be up to 90 feet long and moved faster than running horses.

The Pioneer Historic Byway follows the route of Idaho's pioneers through the town of Franklin and Preston, where you can see many quaint homes and churches now listed on the National Register of Historic Places, and Paris, the home of the Paris Tabernacle.

King's Bowl, a crater 100 feet wide and 150 feet deep, was formed by a prehistoric explosion. It's north of American Falls along Highway 39 at the Great Rift National Landmark.

Idaho is an addiction that isn't negative. Once you've experienced her rugged mountains, sweeping valleys, sheer canyons, and high desert plateaus, you'll want to return again and again. She's truly a precious gem in the crown of this beautiful country we call America.

Snake River at Three Mile Island State Park

Photo Credits

MARY LIZ AUSTIN – *page 43 right; page 51; page 56*

JAMES BLANK – *page 24; page 32 right; page 53; page 64; page 66; page 69; page 72*

TERRY DONNELLY – *front cover; page 29; page 42; page 80;*

DON EASTMAN – *page 20; page 39; page 55 left; page 58; page 65; page 68*

GEORGE WUERTHNER – *page 2; page 6; page 7; page 10; page 11; page 14; page 15; page 17; page 21; page 25; page 28; page 32 left; page 34; page 35; page 38; page 43 left; page 46; page 47; page 50; page 52; page 54; page 55 right; page 57; page 59; page 60; page 61; page 62; page 63; page 73; page 76; page 77; rear cover*

About the Author

Cheryl Landes is a freelance writer who just recently moved to Staten Island, New York, after living in the Pacific Northwest for 22 years. More than 100 of her travel and history articles have been published in U.S. and Canadian magazines, including *Sunset, Northwest Travel, Oregon Coast, Adventure West, Rock and Gem, Old West, Gold Prospector,* and *Postcard Collector.* She works as a technical writer, editor, and indexer at an Internet company in the heart of Manhattan's Financial District.

Beautiful America's Idaho is Landes' second book for Beautiful America Publishing Company. She wrote the second edition of *Beautiful America's Seattle* in 1999.

Henry's Fork of the Snake River in Harriman State Park

Rear Cover: Lost River Range from Big Lost River Valley, near Mackay